A Short Account Of The Life And Conversion Of Sukey Harley, Taken From Her Lips By The Rector's Daughter [- Guise]

When big enough to go out to service, I was hired at a farm house; I made a good servant, I loved work. The farmers were all glad to get me into their houses. I got through such a lot of work, and was as fond of frolic and play. I gave free licence to my tongue. To my shame be it spoken, I could hardly open my mouth but I would fetch an oath; it was dreadful. I married very young. My husband was a very quiet, steady, and sober man; he was never fond of drink, nor of levity of any sort, like the rest of the young men. I used to despise him in my heart, and say, well, what a fool I have got for a husband. He'd just go right on with his work and take no notice of any thing; backwards and forwards, down the lane and up again, to and fro, morning and night, day by day; it was always the same with him. He'd just mind his own business and care for nothing else. Well, I would think with myself, what a dolt my Charles is.

Whenever he heard me curse or swear, he would rebuke me; but very mildly: he used to say, Sukey, I wish I could hear you talk without swearing; I wish you would leave off them words. I was ready to hit him for downright rage. Excepting these bouts, we never had any miss words with each other, and a good reason why, he never gave me any, so then I'd none to give him. Once I remember on a Sunday morning, he said to me, (but very mildly,) Sukey, you ought to get me a clean shirt to put on of a Sunday, and a pair of stockings mended, like any other poor man's wife. I was sadly cut down at this remark, and I thought to myself, well, what an odd fish of a wife I must be not to know this before. I wonder how the other women do. The next Saturday I went round and peeped into all the neighbours' houses; I found the women all busy washing their husbands' and children's things. I was badly hurt to find that I had ne'er treated my husband as well as the rest of the folks. I went home and washed and mended his shirt and stockings: ever after that bout I took care to have a clean shirt and stockings for him against Sunday. I used to make it a practice to go out to the Shop for flour and tea and butter always on the Sunday morning. The woman that kept the shop always told me she did not like it; but I never heeded her. One Sunday, I took Charles along with me to carry some of the things; he made no more profession

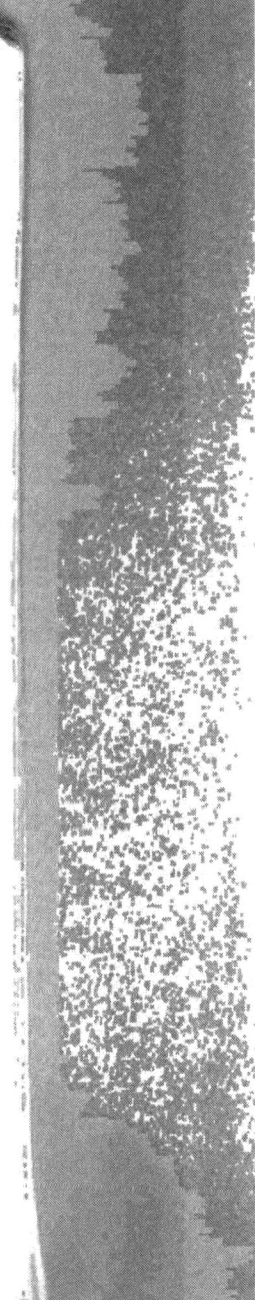

of religion than I did; we were quite ignorant. The woman said again, I wish you would not come on Sunday. Charles would never let me go to the shop on Sundays after that; well, I thought what an oddity man he is, to mind about what the woman says; but we neither of us knew any more about the Sabbath than the beasts of the field.

We went to live at Dorriston; we were very well off; mighty well to live; we kept two pigs; we had enough and to spare; no lack of this world's goods. I made a sight of money, that was all I cared for in this world. I made acquaintance with all the idle, frivolous girls in the village; I should think that there was not the like to be found in all the country; hooting and bawling, shouting, gammocking, and romping. On the Sabbath morning, we used to collect together in a large barn, dancing and revelling, and fooling away the time. I was a very good tuner on the fiddle, and they used to dance. This is the way my Sabbaths were spent. I said to myself, well, it's for the gentlefolks to mind religion, and for such as are fine scholars. I used to wonder sometimes on a Sunday what the folks went to church for. I used to see 'em pass to and fro, and I would like puzzle my mind a bit. Then I would consider, well, that is for the gentlefolks. I was not suffered to take any formalist ways: what I was I was out and out before all, brasen-faced. I have often thought of my brasen face. My disposition was evil; my inclination was evil; my heart and life were evil; the imaginations of my thoughts were evil. I was clean lost, and as insensible as the stones under my feet.

The first thing that gave a turn to my manner of living, was being called on by two women, neighbours, who wished me to go with them to meeting. I refused, but when they came again and pressed me very much, I began to fear they would call me a bad neighbour; so to please them I went. I payed no attention to what was going on there. When I came home, I found that a currant cake I had made for my brother, who was sick at the Black Lion, had been stolen out of my house. This made me so angry, that I said I would ne'er go to meeting any more. The next day came round, and they came again, I was still afraid of being called a bad neighbour, so I yielded and went along with 'em. When I came home, I found that my husband, and house, and all, had like to have been burnt. Charles had set his shirt sleeve on fire, and the flame rose up and caught the timber, and it had all like to have been burnt. Now I was determined I would go no more to meeting, and when the two women came next time, I said, the devil has been at our house, I will ne'er go with you any more. The meeting used to be held at one of the women's houses. But these two would come and pester me to go to church or chapel. I put them off a good while; they still kept teasing me; at last I said, well, I must have a new gown, and a new bonnet, and a new shawl, and then perhaps I may go. I sold my pig, and bought these things, and I went with the women to church next Sabbath. I went two or three times in my new things; the women were almost ashamed of my company, I had dressed myself out such a sight; but they dared not say a word to me, fearing I should leave off going. The devil had fine possession of my heart then; ah! thought I, I am now godly, I'm a right good neighbour now. I made a God of these women, but I hated them, I kept thinking all the while that they were gathered together against me, and so I feared them, so feared of bearing a bad character with them. But I was ignorant of a holy God. I was ignorant of my vileness, my devilish, hellish heart; my sins were hid from my sight, but my God knew me, though I knew not Him, as shall hereafter appear. He chastised me, He chused me, and He began to work in my poor dark soul, though I knew not His hand, yet His hand was with me, lugging me, teasing me, pulling me to Himself, and I scrambling to get away. Oh! blessed be His holy name for ever, it was all His own doing, and He shall have all the honour. I followed the women two or three times to church and chapel in my new things. It was now my trouble began. I soon flung away the new things; it was the devil made me put them on, and it was the devil made me throw them off; he had possession of my heart. At last I went such a sight to church, with my cap all collared and the strings dangling about. Well, the women were ashamed of my company again, just in the other extreme; but they durst not speak about it, I was such an odd woman, so hampered and entangled by the devil and my wicked heart.

This was my trouble, the thought that these women

have got something that I had ne'er got, this was it that troubled me. All day long my thoughts were hampered, my mind was tossicated about this thing ; what have these women got? I wish I knew what they have got. Oh, I was sore distressed ; I was heavily burdened ; I was weary, weary in mind to know somewhat about it. Nothing that ever I heard in church or chapel at that time ever struck my mind. I never paid attention there, my trouble was'nt brought on by the word of man, I could tell no man what ailed me, not even my husband. I did ne'er know, I could ne'er find out myself what was the matter; I would for ever make some light excuse, to know what they two were about. I would peep into old Nancy Smith's door, she would come out, the big tears standing in her eyes, and the book in her hand; well, I hated her; then I'd go to the other, Sukey, she'd say, do come and sit down, and I'll read to you a bit. Well, I'd say, and think to myself, I do hate to come nigh 'em. Then I would look upon her countenance ; O what a blessed look I thought she had in the midst of all her poverty and outward wretched- ness. She was a deal worse off than I, though I am miserable and she is blessed. What does it mean? They must have somewhat; I wish I knew what they have found. Then I'd go home pondering on this matter, puzzling my foolish brains to find out what they'd got; tossed to and fro ; I was weary, weary, weary, day and night, I could find no rest. Oh! I wanted somewhat I could ne'er get. I began to think there must be a God, then I thought, these women know that God. They used to tell me I must pray, so in hopes of knowing their God, I did pray, that is, I said the Lord's Prayer o'er and o'er and o'er again ; this is all the praying I knew. I used to take great notice of the clouds. Well, I'd think, what can it be, is it smoke out of all the chimnies gone and settled there? then again I'd think it can ne'er be smoke. Sometimes they be all cleared off. Well, there must be a God to make these. I now began to be in great terror, it's impossible to say what confused thoughts I had at this time ; no heart but those that have experienced it can tell what dreadful feelings, and tremblings, and shakings pos- sessed my mind.

This was the way my God was leading me to himself. One Sabbath when I was at church, this thought came to my mind, suppose those great big clouds should burst and fall upon my head; suppose this church should fall upon me. Well, I began to be in such terror; then I thought it will not fall down upon those two women; I'll get close against Nancy Rowland, then I shall be safe, I made a great clatter in the church, changing my place, all the folks would stare at me, I was such a poor crack-brained thing. One day I went to Nancy Rowland's as usual to see if I could find out what she had got, she said, Sukey, do come in and stop and take a dish of tea with me; I said well I will. While the kettle was boiling, she read a tract to me, I never paid the least attention to it: not one word could I tell what it was about. Her children came in, she cut 'em each a bit of bread, they took it and seemed thankful, they made their obeisance to me and went off. Then Nancy took and cut me such nice thin slices of bread and butter, honouring me like. I wondered at it, and I looked at her poverty and her rags. Well, I thought, her has got something, I wish I knew what she has got. When I came home, it came into my head to take her some bread and bacon, I cut her ever such a lot and carried it up to her house. I thought she would be glad of it, and would think me such a good neighbour. She seemed to take so little heed of it, she put her hands on the table, and looked up; she was silent; I know now what she was doing, she was giving God thanks, but I then thought she ought to have thanked me more. Ah! how ignorant I was; I went on in this way for three quarters of a year, all beside one fortnight. I was in a dreadful, distressed, tossicated state, the poorest, destitutest creature on the face of the earth, I knew no God, that was the thing that kept me so wretched; I was such a harum-scarum, senseless thing, and very wicked. Nancy Smith would often rebuke me, she lived close up against me, so she heard so much of it. How I would curse and swear at the least thing that put me out of the way. She used to put her head out of the door, and say, oh! Sukey Harley, hell will be your portion; I hated her, I thought she would tell Nancy Rowland, and they would think me a bad neighbour. I would sometimes think of that word, hell, this would fasten on my mind, this must be somewhat dreadful. Some nights I would be afraid of closing my eyes, lest I should tumble into hell.

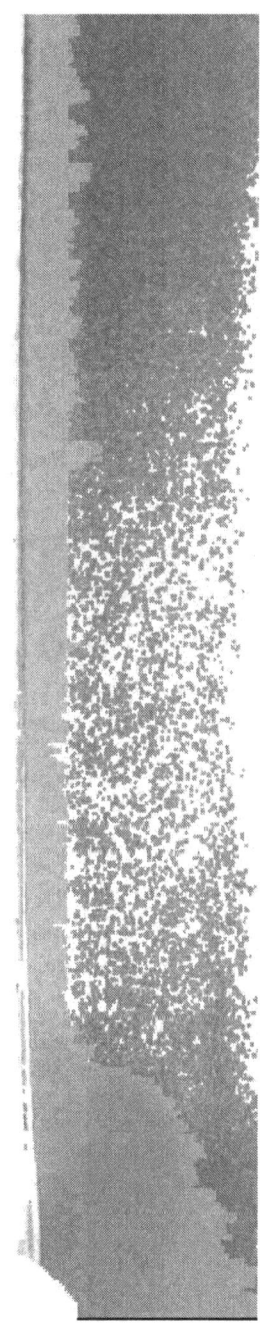

One day I was fluttered about two little pigs, I could not get them into the stye; I cursed and swore at them. As usual, old Nancy Smith came and said, oh! Sukey, Sukey, thee must be born again; I said well, these words confound me; they clean updid me. What can the old hypocrite mean? I soon clapped the pigs into the stye, and went off to Nancy Rowland's, I loved her better than the other, because she was meeker. I said, what do you think that old methodist woman says to me! What? Why, she says, I must be born again! Now, says I, Nancy, how can this be? if it is in the Bible I will believe it; she was silent, but she reached the bible and found the place, and read the words, " Except a man be born again he cannot enter the kingdom of God." Well, did I believe 'em, No, I had not faith, how could I believe? I said, Nancy, how can it be. And which way is it to be done? How is it I never heard this before? Now, suppose my mother is dead, why, what a thing this is, and I never to hear this before. Well, I said, what a lot here is to be done. How I come to this age, six-and-twenty and more, and never been told this before. Well, these words bided with me, I could not get shut on 'em. We must be born again. I had no more understanding of them than a dead corpse. I seemed to be all the while in my confused way to go to God, though, for all, I did not know Him. I did feel that it was only Him that could give me satisfaction. Oh! I thought, if I did but know their God, then I should know all about it. Well, He was lugging me to Himself all the while, but I was so ignorant and foolish, I was as a beast before Him. I often think of that verse, aye, and I am the very same now, just like a beast. Well, I began to grow worse and worse, more full of perplexed thoughts than ever; I was tossed to and fro. What was I to do, I did ne'er know what to do. The reason I dont know God is because I cannot read. Those two women are such fine scholars, they can read such a sight of books. They can pray, they've such a sight of prayers, and I only know this one. Then I thought, I must have a new prayer, the old prayer wont do. I kept repeating it over and over again, but I wanted a new prayer. I mourned, I cried to God to teach me a new prayer; yes, I said to my dear Father in heaven, for He was my Father though I did not know Him; and I cried to Him, and mourned before Him, I begged Him to teach me a new prayer. These words clapped into my mind,—Lord, lead me into the knowledge of thy dear Son,—I never heard about the Son of God, I never knew that God had a Son, yet these words came into my heart; it was the prayer God taught me Himself, no one else taught me. I never, never heard what those two women would be bantering me about. I was so tossicated with my own thoughts, I paid no heed to their words. The Lord put those words into my heart. I seemed quite rejoiced that their God had taught me. He had eked out my prayer a little longer, for I still kept saying the Lord's prayer, and added those new words to the end of it. I never coveted any fresh words after this. Well, I prayed this new prayer for about a fortnight. On the Sunday night after the fortnight, I went with the women to chapel, I was in a dreadful, awful state. Oh! what a dreadful state I was in, I thought I was going to hell, and I counted nine other women in the chapel that I thought would come with me. Those two, I thought, would go to heaven; they were for none of my company. This was what I was thinking counting the people, putting them, which I thought were for heaven, and which were for hell. Myself, I thought, was sure to go to hell, but I thought I had not yet done enough to go to hell, then a dreadful thought came into my head, I wonder if I can find Charles' knife; suppose I were to kill him; suppose I were to kill my child. Oh! I were in a dreadful, awful state that night at chapel. When we came out, I got close behind those two women. I was afear'd the clouds would fall down upon my head, I was just like a crazy thing. I heard the old woman say to the other, O Nancy, Nancy, there's some precious soul called to night. Ah! who should it be but me. Yet I knew it not; I said to myself, what does that old methodist fool mean? When I got home, I went into my dismal heartless way. I thought I was going to hell, where was the use of my praying any more. I was tempted to give in praying, I thought I should ne'er know their God. Before I went to bed, I got into the dark corner, as usual I began in my way to pray these words, I thought I felt the devil pulling me by the hair of the head, yet I held fast by the table. I was afear'd to go to sleep that night, I thought I should tumble into hell, and that thought about Charles' knife troubled me.

On the monday morning while I was eating my breakfast (but I had no stomach to eat,) it was after Charles was
gone to work, these words entered into my mind, " Behold
I stand at the door and knock, if any man hear my voice ·
and open the door, I will come in unto him, and sup with
him, and be with him, and he with me." I said this is
the text the man had for his sermon last night ; well it was,
but I had ne'er heard it then. I heard it now, though all
the words quite plain came into my heart. Oh! I thought
suppose it should be their God at the door. Oh! how
joyful I would get up and loose him the door. Now I
thought, I can ne'er give in praying, those words have so
encouraged me, I went up the ladder into my bed room,
and began to pray. I made such a noise the folks might
have heard me in the street. I was afear'd I should
frighten my child ; I came down and looked at her, she
was a little one eating her breakfast. I went up again
and did not stop long. I came down again, and filled the
child's bag with meat, and sent her off to school ; I put
her out at the door and locked and bolted it. Then I said
in my own strength, I will never open this door again 'till
I know their God. I stuffed the windows with all the old
rags I could find, I could not bear the light ; then I went
down on my kness in the dark corner and began praying
these same words that I had used to do, the same words
over and over and over again,—the Lord's prayer, and
Lord, lead me into the true knowledge of thy dear Son.
I felt as if I would have pulled the roof over my head, I
went tearing and tearing at it with such vehement earnest-
ness. Well, who put that strong cry into my heart?
Was it from myself? No ; but He gave it me and forced
me to cry out, because it was His own blessed will to hear
me and answer me. I felt him come ; it's past my talking
about such a wonderful time ; it's clear past telling. No
words can express the feelings of my heart at this time.
He fetched me of my knees ; I started up, I cannot find
words to express the wonderful doings of that blessed
moment : well, this is past. He showed me all my sins
that I had committed even from a child. Yes, that bit of
pink ribbon I had stolen for my doll's cap, came upon me.
He showed me how for that one sin I might have been
sent to hell, and he would have been just. Oh! He
showed me my black desert, how I had deserved to go to

ell; what a reprobate I had been, and how like a devil I
ad walked upon the earth; how I had angered Him with
ny sinfulness. My heavy sins and my vileness came upon
ne. Oh! He appeared such a holy God, such a heavenly,
bright and glorious Being; suppose He had said to me
hen at that awful moment, " Depart from me ye cursed,"
He would have been just, and to hell I must have gone.

Oh! what a holy God mine is. Well, I was lost, I
could ne'er tell what to do; lost in wonder, lost in surprise;
yet all this time He kept me from being frightened. I had
been frightened, but not now, there was somewhat that
held me from being frightened. He seemed to tell me all
my sins were forgiven. I had such a sight inwardly of my
dear Redeemer's sufferings; how He was crucified, how
He hung on the cross for me; it was as if He showed me
what I deserved, yet He seemed to say, He had suffered
that desert; it was as if He made it so plain to me, how
that He would save me, because it was His own blessed
will to save me. It was as if he had shown me how He
had chosen me from the foundation of the world. He
would have mercy on me because He would have mercy.

I never knew what sin was till now, but He showed
me what it was; how black, how dreadful. I felt it was
my just desert to go to hell. He would have been just
and holy to send me there. I was so lost in wonder, that
I said, O Lord Jesus Christ, make hell ten thousand times
hotter before thou sendest me there. These were my
very words. I can tell the words, but the feeling I cannot
tell. But He saved me, till I was so overwhelmed that I
did not know what to do. I can truly say, since that
blessed morning, I have a Saviour and a Redeemer, yes, I
have; ever since that blessed time, my dear and heavenly
Father has kept me in His dear hands, and guided me and
counselled me Himself. Well, I went and unblocked the
windows, cleared away all the dirty rags, and let in the
blessed light of the sun, the glorious light, my Father's
light. I unbolted the door and opened it, I looked out;
what a glorious light, I saw my God in every thing; the
clouds, those clouds I had so often puzzled over; my God
was in the clouds, the trees, the hedges, the fields, the
beasts of the field, the birds of the air, showed me that I
had a God. All things were new to me, I was unbound,
I was loosed; yes, I wondered at it. I went to old Nancy

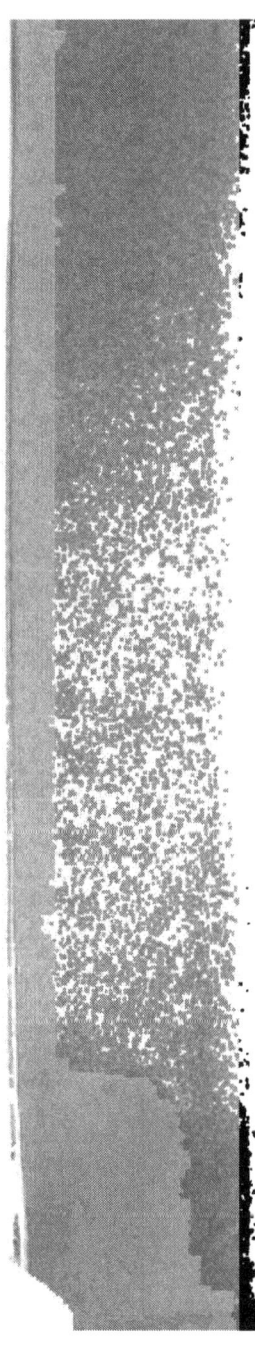

Smith's door and looked in, I could not speak; she said,
Sukey, what's the matter? I could make no answer; off
I ran to the other, I was enabled to tell her somewhat, but
very little, I could not find words to express the goodness
of God to me. I knew, understood and believed these
words, "Ye must be born again." This blessed state
continued a good while, I felt the happiest creature, the
joyfullest woman on the face of the earth. My God
enabled me from that very time to break loose from all my
vain companions in the flesh; they thought it very hard,
yes, and so did I too, but my heavenly dear Father called
me out from them, and I followed Him, I dared not do
otherwise; I was set then off at a distance from them;
ever since that blessed morning I have been a lone soul on
the face of the earth, "A sparrow alone upon the house
top." I often think of that verse, it suits me. It was no
great while after this, I had a desire to read; I longed to
read the blessed words for myself. I got my little wench
to teach me the letters; she used to grow sleepy, so I
would give her two suppers to encourage her; all the
while I was praying to my God to enable me to learn; she
brought me on as far as this—God is love, God is light;
and these very words came over me, when I spelt out the
words, they came into my heart. I thought my God is
love, He is light, He can teach me Himself. I wanted no
more teaching of Mary; from that time I would take my
book, and go down on my knees, and look up to my
heavenly Father, and beg of Him to teach me. I used to
spell out the words, and then look up to know how to call
them. Oh! how I felt at these times; I can give no
description of my feelings, but I had this confidence given
me, that He would teach me to read His blessed Word,
and He did teach me; it was surprising how He put the
words into my mind and memory; yes, I can truly say,
"I have been taught of God."

It was during this time we removed to where we now
live, Pulverback. I have known heavy seasons of sorrow,
great darkness, bitter distress, I have been sorely tempted
of Satan, and plagued with the corruptions of my own
heart; O, what heavy temptations I have been under for
days and days together; I have just sat still on my chair,
tempted and buffetted of Satan; I have not had the least
power to do one hand's turn for my own defence; a poor,

helpless creature, straitened, weary thing; sorely tempted
to believe that I had sinned against the Holy Ghost. Oh!
the fiery darts of the evil one, they have pierced my poor
soul through and through. Yes, I know what sore temptations mean, yet in all this my God has been with me
still. He has never left me nor forsaken me. It is my
God who teaches me to profit. It is Him who comforts
me. He sends down His Holy Spirit into my heart, and
brings my dear Redeemer's sufferings to my remembrance,
then I can bear all; this is the thing that bears me up in
the midst of all my sorrows. Oh! how He reveals my
Saviour to me. Yes, I can truly say, I have known Christ
on earth; I have known Him from a babe; from the
manger to the cross. The nails, the thorns, the spear,—
my sins pierced him then. Oh! when He brings these
things upon me, my hard heart is melted; then I can
mourn; the enemy is then vanquished; he shirks off; my
Jesus comes into my soul. If Christ were not to come
into my soul, what a blundering devil and heart here would
be together. He chastens and cuts me with one hand,
and strengthens and comforts me with the other. Oh!
the tender mercies of my God to me. He blesses His
word to my soul; He corrects me; He chastens me in
love; and He orders my way before Him, and sends down
His Holy Spirit to comfort me. Oh! bless and praise His
holy name for ever. I ever bless the Lord for sending me
some books. They do come from Him. That hymn you
have been reading it's all the very same as the Lord
teaches me in my soul. Hart's hymns, now these are
my life; Hart understood my life. Now the enemy, and
my deceitful heart have torn and cut asunder my soul.
How I've been past every thing pestered about this. I'd
think with myself, well, am I right, I'm like no one else,
they be all so quiet, so sleek, so smooth; they seem to
have nothing of the buffettings, and strivings, and tossings,
and turmoilings, and mournings, and groanings, that I
have; what does this mean? Be I a christian? Am I
in the right road? Why canna' I live in quietness like
other good christian people. When the devil comes in,
he would tell me I was clean contrary to the people of
God. Such a fuss with my prayers; such a mourning;
such darkness, such sorrow, this been ne'er the walk of a
christian. A christian been all in the light. He donna'

c

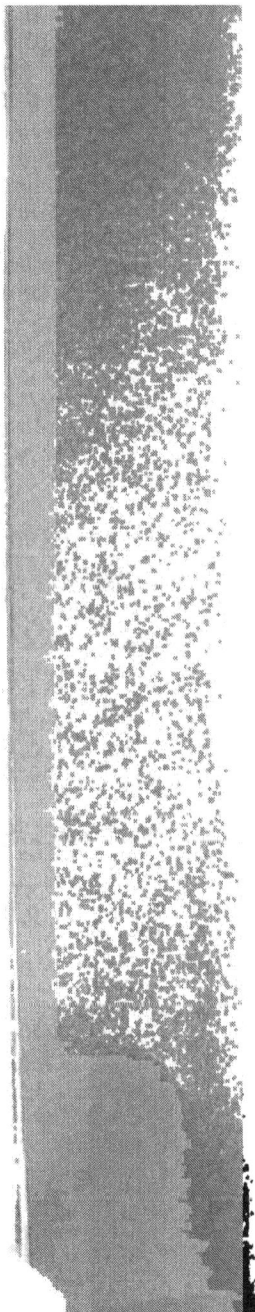

find such a heap of wickedness in his heart like what I've got. Oh! what I have suffered for years, aye, for years. Then I'd cry to the Lord, O my dear Heavenly Father, do resolve these heavy doubts and fears, do please to lead me into the right road.

He'd make me feel how that all my strength must come from him. "Without me ye can do nothing." I believe those words. Once when I was in great darkness, this was brought to my mind, "Lean entirely on Him to go the road He directs, through temptations, through sorrows, through darkness, and trust entirely on Him." I'd think again, but how is it? I can never find one person to understand my feelings, they be all so different, clean contrary, sure if they knew my God, they would all know my life. Now this is the way I have been tossicated for years.

I read Bradford's Letter, 20th, which is as follow:—
To a faithful woman in heaviness,

"How should God wipe away tears from your eyes in heaven, if now on earth you shed no tears? How would heaven be a place of rest, if you found it rest on earth? How could you desire to be at home, if in your journey you found no grief? How could you so often call upon God, and talk with Him, if your enemy slept all day long? How should you elsewhere be made like unto Christ—I mean in joy,—if you sob not with Him in sorrow? If you will have joy and felicity, you must have sorrow and misery. If you will go to heaven, you must scan by hell. If you will embrace Christ in his robes, you must not scorn Him in His rags. If you will sit at Christ's table in His kingdom, you must first abide by Him in His temptations. If you will partake of His glory, forsake not His cup of ignominy."

O what a precious letter. Did you say that man lived three hundred years ago? Well, the Lord has had a people on earth from the beginning. Now when that dear man wrote the letter, the Lord knew how it would fetch comfort into my sorrowful soul so many years after. It was His doing, it was the Lord who instructed him, and taught him in the things in that letter, and it is Him who sent it to refresh my soul.

I was talking with my niece, her parents were Ranters: I said, Emma, I have heard your people say, you must give God your heart. Now tell me, did you ever give God your heart? She said, why, aye, I have. Then I tell you, Emma, I never have. Why, Aunt, I donna' know what to think of you now. What, have you never given God your heart? No, I said I did not give it Him, but He took it though. What, against your will? He made me willing, otherwise I had never given it Him. Why aunt, said Emma, you are one by yourself. Aye, my dear wench, I am one by myself, and I am well reconciled that it should be so, because I find very few indeed who know any thing like my experience, and so I must be one by myself. I tell you, Emma, the unchanged sinner can never begin to turn to God. My aunt, she said again, you are one by yourself, and that's how it is. I can tell you but little, but this I will tell you, I was not converted by man, nor yet by my own power, but by the Spirit of God. I love them that talk that the Lord teaches. I love to hear them relate what the Lord has done for their souls. We cannot receive the light of life from man, it must be the gift of God. O, Emma, it's a great work, it's too great for a poor, blind, wretched sinner to undertake for himself. Our God is just and holy, a glorious, wonderful Being. Now can such a black, vile sinner as I stand before Him? He must fit me. He must do all the work. I cannot do one hand's turn for myself, there must be no intermixture. Yea, and He will do it all, and He shall have all the glory. Ask, by prayer, Emma, that God would be pleased to give you repentance unto life into the sinner's heart. Emma, did you ever feel cursed pride cling round your heart when you pray? No, Aunt. Then I tell you, Emma, you are not like me. That pride, it's the biggest enemy I've got. My proud heart! oh, my proud heart! how I mourn on account of my proud heart, and thus I appear like one alone. Yes, I am like one by myself, and when I am alone I am alone, for I am clean lost, then the poorest, the helplessest thing; but the Lord donna' leave me long alone neither. He comes and draws my heart up to Himself, and this is all I have got to say, the Lord is my sure confidence, and my trust, and He shall have all the glory.

Sukey Harley's feelings when her house was burning.

It was Sunday Morning, I was sitting all alone by myself. My husband and child were gone to church. I was very poorly in body, and sore distressed in mind. I had the devil with me, he had been with me for several days. He had been tempting me all manner of ways; he had been trying to pull away my faith. My sins lay heavy on my heart, very heavy. My heavy sins, ever since the day of my conversion, terrified my conscience, and afflicted me, and pressed sore upon me; they were a heavy burden, too heavy for me. My Saviour had hid His face. His precious blood was clean out of my sight. My sinful, wicked heart and the crafty devil, were all the company I had, we were shut up in the house together. I lived in a lone house; no one lived within half a mile of me besides one man, named John Morgan, who lived under the same roof, in another part of the house. He had gone out early in the morning, and left a large fire in the grate. The enemy was tempting me all manner of ways, and I almost believed him; he told me that my God had clean forsaken me, and that my blessed Jesus had hid His blessed face from me for ever. He said that I was never a child of God; that I had been all these years in a delusion; that my sins were too great to be pardoned; that I had sinned against pardoning; that the just and holy God would never call me His child. I was too filthy, too polluted a wretch to be noticed by Him; and all manner of things he crammed into my sinful, guilty heart. One thing he said, was, that against March, when the high winds blow, the house would be blown down, and I tumbled into hell. Well, he had the upper hand of me, and I was sorely sifted in my spirit, and had not one word to answer to him because I felt myself so cursed. O what a woeful plight I was in on that dismal morning. I thought, well, what a thing this is. Is it true? Have I been all these years in a delusion? Just as I was thinking this, I perceived the smell of burning. The house filled with smoke, and I said, what, is the house on fire? I was so very weak and poorly, I could hardly crawl to the door. I looked out and I saw the roof of my house all on fire. Now the devil triumphed; he told me, and he almost made me believe it too, that this would never have happened to me if I had been a child of God; he really made it out so clear, that this disaster could not have befallen one of the elect children of God, that I was clean driven beside myself. What, he said, dont you think God would defend one of His own children? You are none of His; you have been in a delusion all these years.

Oh! what a dismal condition I was in then. I durst not look up, no I durst not; I hardly dare cry for help; I knew the holy and righteous God was just and righteous in all His ways, and I thought I had been offending His glorious Majesty all these years. I was such a black, foul wretch, how dared I call Him Father.

I stood upon the causeway, and kept looking at my burning house; but from that day to this, I could never describe the deadly sickness, the frightful terror that seized my inmost soul. Oh! it is very solemn to speak of. I believed the devil's lies when he told me that God would never have suffered this to happen to one of His children; yes, I did believe it, and took it for a real sign and standing proof that I was right down deceived in all my blessed hopes, and that I should never be found among the true elect children of God; and, as I stood looking at the fire, I cried out with an exceeding bitter cry, I cried out with a loud voice, and said, I am undone, I am lost, I am undone for ever.

Was it my house I cared for? No, but it was because I thought all my heavenly and golden treasures were lost. Then I fell down all along upon the grassy bank before my burning house. I had no power either to attempt to save any thing myself, or to call for assistance; as for going into the burning house, I dared not do it, I thought the flames were ready to devour me, and I was the guiltiest wretch, my sins, my black sins, were ready to swallow me up; I kept lamenting my woeful case. What, I said, is this true? Have I been all these years in a delusion? Is my blessed hope come to nought at last? Is my precious Saviour clean gone for ever? Will He be favourable no more? Will He be no longer my Father, my Redeemer? O, what shall I do? When I began to think what a blessed confidence I had had in Him, and how I thought He had told me Himself, that I should be His child, and that He would save me and be a Father to me, and an Almighty Redeemer. Then I began to think what a boast I had made of Him, and how I had published abroad to all the world that I had got a Saviour and a God; and now I thought, is it all gone to this, what, is all my hope gone? O, what shall I do? Then I began to think what blessed things He had done for me. Why, said I to myself, I thought He had been pleased to reveal His name

c 3

in me, and teach me to read His word, and call Him my Saviour, and now has it been a delusion? How can this be, did He not teach me to pray to Him, and has He not times and times blessed His word to me? And was it not Himself who taught me to read His word? I thought it was Him, I thought He had done all these things for me, and now is He going to forsake me? O, my woeful case, my sins, my heavy sins, my black sins. O, this is what has done it, this is what has done it, and I cried out like David, yes, I roared out this disquietness of my soul.

I suppose if any one had come along and seen me lying all along upon the grass, and my house on fire, they would have thought me a desperate fool, and so I was, the devil's fool. But what could they have known about that? That's not the way they would have put it. They would have said, why not go and pull the things out of the house, what is the use of lying and crying there, go and get assistance, and try and save what you can. O, they know nothing at all about it, my heavenly, my blessed, my only hope was now gone, and what good would man's assistance do me. What did I care for my house? What did I care for all the things that were in it; let them burn, let them burn. How can I take thought for them. My God is gone, my sins have driven Him away. What is all the world to me in this hour of darkness? All is loss, and dross; my house is in the shadow of death.

Well, I kept crying, and bemoaning, and lamenting, myself thus; I hardly dared to look up to God for help, I thought He was clean gone, I almost feared for ever. My sins had hid His mercy from me, and Satan told me my hope was gone for ever; all was lost. Ah! but it was not lost though, that was a lie. The blessed and merciful Lord in heaven, He heard my dolorous cry. Blessed for ever be His most holy and glorious Name, He heard my pitiful cry, He saw my tears; He had compassion on me in His own time, He came to my relief, He darted into my soul in one moment, yes, in one moment he darted into my soul. He rebuked the tempter. Then was the devil vanquished. The blessed Jesus put him to flight in a moment. And the blessed Jesus took possession of my sorrowful soul. He brought joy in turn of my heavy sorrow. He assured me over and over again that He was my Saviour and my Deliverer, and that He would never leave me nor forsake me. I felt His precious blood sufficient to wash away all my sins, and my soul was joyful in God my Saviour.

He strengthened me marvellously; it is impossible for me to describe rightly the wondrous change He wrought upon me, I who was so weak, so poorly, that I had been hardly able to crawl out of the house, and to throw myself on the grass, in one moment was strengthened and invigorated, and replenished with all I stood in need of. Then I banged into the burning house, I cared neither for flames nor burning rafters, nor timbers, nor yet for the devil, my mortal foe, for my Saviour was with me, He was my defence. O, how safe I was! How safe I felt in Him! He and I were alone together in the burning house.

Well, first I got hold of my box of books, where my precious bible was, and I flung it out of the window into the garden, then I went up stairs and heaved up the tub where the bacon was; I had been salting a pig that week, it was as much as two men could have carried down stairs, the flitches and hams lay together in the tub. I bore it up with the strength the Lord had given me, and by His help I carried it down stairs, and took it out of the house and set it in the garden. Then I went to the clock and lifted it up and carried it out. Then again up stairs, and began to throw out the bedding; and next I set myself to unscrew the bedstead, while I was doing that John M—— who had seen the flames at a distance, came running out of breath to my assistance. Poor fellow, he came ringing his hands, and making such a do. Oh! Sukey, Sukey, what a bad job this is. How did this happen? What shall I do? Oh! poor fellow, if he could but have understood; but he could not have understood if I had told him. This was no bad job for me, for by it I proved the tender mercies of God to me unworthy. We soon got the bedstead down; then John went to the corner cupboard, in it there were cups and saucers and all kinds of crockery ware; and there was a small jug of milk which had been given me in the morning. There was no time to take any thing out of the cupboard, but John tore it away by main strength, dragging hooks and staples and all along with it out of the wall. Just as he had done this, there came crowds of people hastening to the place, they had seen the flames at a distance, just as they were coming out of church,

and men, women, and children, all in a throng, hurried to the spot. I had enough of helpers then. Ah! but it was the Lord who had done all for me. He had brought that sweet comfort into my soul, or what good would such as them have done me.

We soon got the house cleared. No one dared to attempt to save any thing out of John Morgan's house, for the fire having began on his side of the house, the flames had reached too high before it was discovered. The people were all satisfied about it. I lost one small three-legged table, which I had lent him. Besides that, there was not one thing missing of all my goods. This was how the Lord would have it. It was all His doing. I hardly know what I was about all this time I was saving my goods, my soul was so joyful in God my Saviour. I was clean beside myself to think of His wondrous love to me, unworthy, black, polluted, hell-deserving sinner.

When all the goods were out of the house, and the roof fell in, and the flames rose up, and the smoke, then I looked and wondered at it. It was a fearful sight to think what my sins had deserved, and what a deliverance the Lord had brought me. My soul had been just ready to fall into the lowest hell, and He stretched out His hand and plucked me from the burning. What great salvation He sent to my poor soul in that hour of darkness; I could take no thought about my poor body, but now He took care of that, and saved for me those worldly things, which in that hour of darkness I could take no thought about. Bless the Lord, O my soul.

When the people saw all the things I had carried out single-handed, they looked and wondered; there were many more things than what are named in this paper. My memory would not serve to tell them all, the loaves of bread, and pork pies, a whole peck of flour, I got them all out of the house together, but how or which way I did it I cannot tell; but this I know, when I came to look at the loads of things I had brought out by myself, I truly wondered at it, and so did the people. Why Sukey, they said, you never brought out that, and you never carried out this; What, all by yourself? No, No, I might have said to them, but they could not have understood me, I did it, No, it was my God. He carried the things for me. And this I know, for I had not the least power that ever was, till He sent that wonderful strength into my soul, aye, and into my body too; so by this, I know that it was His doing; I was wholly taken up and lifted out of myself with the abundance of consolation which had flowed into my soul by His restoring to me those blessed and heavenly things which I thought had fled for ever. I was taking no thought for my poor body, or earthly goods, all the while I was carrying my goods out of the house. It was surely the Lord who kept me alive that day in the midst of the fire. Yes, He kept me alive and gave me life, both bodily and spiritually; so I say, let Him have all the praise.

When I came to open the corner cupboard, not a single cup was chipped, nor the least thing broken or spoiled in any way. And there was the jug of milk standing on the shelf exactly as I had put it in on the morning, not one drop spilled upon the board. Well, at the sight of that jug of milk, how His mercies came afresh into my mind, to think that He should put forth His hand to save my jug of milk, and the people all saw it and wondered at it, but as for me, I knew how it was; it was the blessed Lord's doing, to teach my soul His tender mercies.

Pulverback, Shrewsbury, Aug. 2nd, 1836.

To Mr. Bourne, from Sukey Harley.

Hoping that he is my dear brother in the Lord. You ask me, Sir, if I am able to perceive many changes in my mind. Yes, I should think I have; when darkness comes and God hides his face, dear I feel so distressed, so distressed; it's dreadful to be without God; I cry till He comes down. My Jesus comes to me, I cannot go to Him; I mourn, I cry, it's all the trouble I know, when my God hides His face it is not for long at a time; I could not live sometimes an hour, sometimes two, not for a whole day. It's very seldom a whole day, perhaps, but God visits me some part of it. He seldom goes for long at a time; it's dreadful sickness, yes, that's my heavy trouble. When He comes to me again, He takes all trouble away; all distressed thoughts, let the sorrow be what it will. He comes in the midst of all, turns all to joy, nothing can hurt me. It's the devil, and the old-dwelling sin make the sorrow; the devil claps in, all joy is gone then, but Jesus comes and drives away the devil; then what joy I have,

what comfort, when I can look up. Do you want a verse as suits me at such times as these, this is one:

> Beyond my utmost wants,
> His love and power can bless;
> To praying souls he always grants
> More than they can express.

My heart was very hard last Saturday; well, I could na' break it, I could na' melt it; I mourned, I grieved. When my Redeemer came, He did it, He melted my hard heart. I found such a place of scripture this morning, I felt as though every word was written to me. " Thou shalt remember all the way which the Lord thy God has led thee these forty years in the wilderness, to humble thee, to prove thee, to know what was in thine heart," Oh! I read these words, I mean the whole chapter; they were spoken to me, I gave them to my husband, I gave them to my daughter; I marked these words in my Bible, I would wish to remember these words and to mark them for ever. I must tell you, Sir, the mercies of my God to me. His tender mercies; how He blessed His word to me. It's very precious when the Lord blesses His word to my soul. Sir, you speak about my talking to others, I am this sort of woman, I canna' speak nothing till my Jesus comes and puts words into my mouth; then I can speak, O yes, I can speak then. You say the grace of God in you is something. But I'm the ignorantest, poorest creature, I canna' find a place in the Bible, I canna' find one verse, I canna' find one hymn, nor nothing; this is what I am, Sir; I do na' forget poor sinners, when the Lord bids me I can talk to one or another; but till He bids me I dare not open my mouth. What I speak to them is according to my own experience. I tell them the truth; when I have liberty from the God of heaven then I can go; I can go without any fear then; I donna' fear man, I want nothing else, but liberty from the Lord; if He donna' give me liberty I am dumb; I canna' speak one word.

O, where our precious Saviour has not been working, what a destitute place our world is. They throw it by, I see them tremble when I have told them my experience; I see them tremble, but they throw it by; what a master Satan is. I was chained up, fast bound in his chain, till my blessed Redeemer broke the chain, then I was loosed.

Lightning Source UK Ltd.
Milton Keynes UK
UKHW020621260719

346866UK00004B/266/P